by Jim Gigliotti

Consultant: Starshine Roshell
Music and Entertainment Journalist
Santa Barbara, CA

New York, New York

Credits
Cover, © Wenn US/Alamy Stock Photo; 4, © WENN Ltd./Alamy Stock Photo; 5, © ZUMA Press, Inc./Alamy Stock Photo; 6, © Kevin Mazur/WireImage for MTV/Getty Images; 7, © Catherine McGann/Getty Images; 8–9, © ZUMA Press, Inc./Alamy Stock Photo; 10, © Seth Poppel/Yearbook Library; 11, © Pete Mariner/Retna/Photoshot/Newscom; 12, © Cal Vornberger/Alamy Stock Photo; 13, © Lester Cohen/WireImage/Getty Images; 14, Wikimedia; 15, © David J. Hogan/Getty Images; 16L, © Phil McCarten/UPI/Newscom; 16–17, © ZUMA Press, Inc./Alamy Stock Photo; 18L, © Gary Null/NBC/NBCU Photo Bank via Getty Images; 18–19, © Rich Kane/Icon SMI/Newscom; 20L, © Monika Graff/UPI/Newscom; 20–21, © Matt Sayles/Invision/AP; 22T, © Phil McCarten/UPI/Newscom; 22B, © Warongdech/Dreamstime; 23T, © Phil McCarten/UPI/Newscom; 23B, © Rich Kane/Icon SMI/Newscom.

Publisher: Kenn Goin
Creative Director: Spencer Brinker
Production and Photo Research: Shoreline Publishing Group LLC

Library of Congress Cataloging-in-Publication Data

Names: Gigliotti, Jim, author.
Title: Bruno Mars / by Jim Gigliotti.
Description: New York, New York : Bearport Publishing, [2018] | Series: Amazing Americans: pop music stars | Includes bibliographical references and index.
Identifiers: LCCN 2017045546 (print) | LCCN 2017045588 (ebook) | ISBN 9781684025176 (ebook) | ISBN 9781684024599 (library)
Subjects: LCSH: Mars, Bruno, 1985-—Juvenile literature. | Musicians—United States—Biography—Juvenile literature.
Classification: LCC ML3930.M318 (ebook) | LCC ML3930.M318 G54 2018 (print) | DDC 782.42164092 [B] —dc23
LC record available at https://lccn.loc.gov/2017045546

For more information, write to Bearport Publishing Company, Inc., 45 West 21st Street, Suite 3B, New York, New York 10010. Printed in the United States of America.

10 9 8 7 6 5 4 3 2 1

CONTENTS

Music Superstar

Bruno Mars danced across the stage, singing one of his biggest hits. The crowd went wild. His fans clapped their hands and stomped their feet. They sang along with the **lyrics**. Clearly, they loved every move he made!

A fan takes a selfie with Bruno.

Seven of Bruno's songs have been No. 1 hits!

Island Born

Bruno Mars was born in Honolulu, Hawaii, on October 8, 1985. His real name is Peter Gene Hernandez. His dad gave him the nickname "Bruno." When he started his **career**, Bruno chose Mars as his last name.

Bruno and his dad, Peter, in 2013

Bruno and his mom in 1990

Why did Bruno choose the name "Mars"? Because, he says, "girls think I'm out of this world!"

Born to Dance

Bruno began performing with his family when he was four years old. He loved being on stage. Bruno was a born **showman**. Even before he learned to sing, crowds loved to watch him dance!

Bruno performed with his family in a group called The Love Notes.

Bruno's sisters are Tahiti, Jaime, Presley, and Tiara. They became singers, too.

The Natural

Surprisingly, Bruno never took singing or dancing lessons. He also didn't need lessons to learn to play a musical instrument. Instead, he easily learned to play on his own.

In high school, Bruno formed a band called The School Boys.

Bruno's 2003 high school senior yearbook photo

Bruno's talents make him an exciting performer.

California Dreaming

After high school in 2003, Bruno moved to Los Angeles. There, he started writing songs for other performers. Still, he kept working hard on his own music. "You can't knock on opportunity's door and not be ready!" he said.

Bruno has written songs for stars such as CeeLo Green (left).

Bruno has also written songs for singer Alicia Keys.

The First Hit

In 2009, Bruno wrote a song with Travie McCoy called "Nothin' on You." Rapper B.o.B. recorded it. Bruno got to sing some of the lyrics on the record. It wasn't long before everyone wanted to know the new singer's name. Bruno was on his way to stardom.

The cover of B.o.B.'s album

In 2010, Bruno formed a band called The Hooligans.

Tour Time

In 2010, Bruno released his first album, *Doo-Wops & Hooligans*. It was a huge hit! Soon after, he went on a concert tour. Most of his performances sold out right away. Everyone wanted to see Bruno!

In 2011, Bruno won a Grammy Award. It was for a song on *Doo-Wops & Hooligans* called "Just the Way You Are."

Bruno sings songs from *Doo-Wops & Hooligans* on a TV show in 2010.

Music Mix

Bruno performs many different kinds of music! His **genres** include rhythm and blues (R&B), funk, rap, hip-hop, pop, and soul. He has been inspired by Elvis Presley, Prince, and many other musicians.

Elvis Presley's music and dancing have inspired Bruno.

Bruno and The Hooligans play at halftime during the Super Bowl in 2014.

Bruno also performed at the 2016 Super Bowl.

Top of the Charts

In November 2016, Bruno released his third album. It was called *24K Magic*. Bruno's smooth voice and clever songs made the album another **smash** hit. The sky is the limit for a performer who is "out of this world"!

Bruno with two trophies from the MTV Music Video Awards

On tour, Bruno sings songs from his album *24K Magic*. The numeral XXIV on his hat means "24."

Bruno's *24K Magic* tour will visit 34 countries in 2017 and 2018.

Timeline

Here are some key dates in Bruno Mars's life.

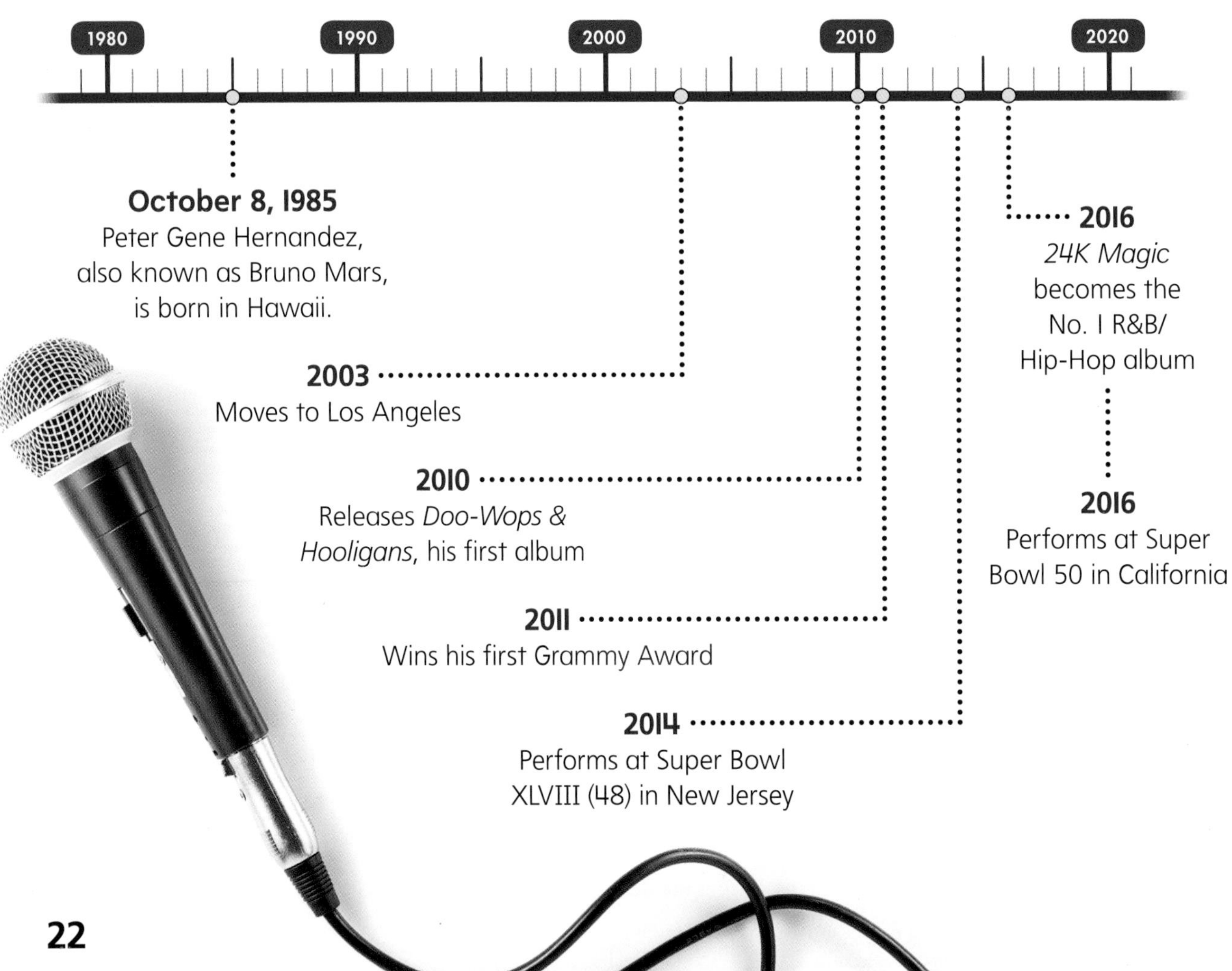

October 8, 1985
Peter Gene Hernandez, also known as Bruno Mars, is born in Hawaii.

2003
Moves to Los Angeles

2010
Releases *Doo-Wops & Hooligans*, his first album

2011
Wins his first Grammy Award

2014
Performs at Super Bowl XLVIII (48) in New Jersey

2016
Performs at Super Bowl 50 in California

2016
24K Magic becomes the No. 1 R&B/Hip-Hop album

Glossary

career (kuh-RIHR) a job path

genres (ZHAN-ruhs) styles or kinds of music

Grammy (GRAMM-ee) an award that recognizes the best music each year

lyrics (LEER-iks) the words of a song

showman (SHO-man) a performer skilled at holding an audience's attention

smash (SMASH) something in entertainment that is very popular

Index

Read More

Brown, Risa. *Bruno Mars (Robbie Reader Contemporary Biographies).* Hallandale, FL: Mitchell Lane (2015).

Morganelli, Adrianna. *Bruno Mars (Superstars!).* New York: Crabtree (2013).

Learn More Online

To learn more about Bruno Mars, visit
www.bearportpublishing.com/AmazingAmericans

About the Author

Jim Gigliotti is a former editor at the National Football League. He now writes books on a variety of topics for young readers.